piano • vocal • guitar

THE SONGS OF DON McLEAN

CW00525703

Cover Photo: DAVID GAHR

ISBN 0-7935-0070-2

HAL•LEONARD®
CORPORATION
7777 W. BLUEMOUND RD. P.O. BOX 13819 MILWAUKEE, WI 53213

Visit Hal Leonard Online at
www.halleonard.com

"Don McLean is the most singular and durable of all of our popular vocalists and writers"

Nat Hentoff, jazz critic

"Don McLean has survived the slings and arrows of outrageous fortune with characteristic wit and wisdom"

Don Heckman,
L.A. Times 1990

"Don McLean's picking as much as his singing is par excellence"

Eric Clapton

"20 years ago Don McLean's style helped start things for both McLean and the singer-songwriter movement of the 1970s"

Mike Toombs,
San Diego Union 1990

Photo: Peter Nash

THE SONGS OF DON McLEAN

In an era of so much disposable pop, the longevity of Don McLean's musical quality is especially notable. His insightful material, from original songs to unique interpretations of classics, has given his long career a great sense of continuity and intelligence, and won him enduring respect all around the world.

Born in New Rochelle, New York in 1945, Don McLean grew up with such wide-ranging musical inspirations as Buddy Holly, The Weavers and Frank Sinatra, and had performed on numerous stages by the time he reached his teens. Concurrently attending Villanova University (where he was part of the folk scene that included his friend Jim Croce) and Iona College (where he graduated), Don continued to perform at as many clubs and concerts as possible.

In 1968, McLean sang at a benefit for the Hudson River Sloop Restoration with his friend Pete Seeger, and later that year was picked to be the "Hudson River Troubadour" by the New York State Council on the Arts. For six weeks he travelled the length of the river, playing three concerts a day, five days a week, in almost every town along the Hudson. At the same time McLean started playing concerts, opening for Josh White, Blood, Sweat and Tears, Richie Havens, Three Dog Night, Steppenwolf and others.

He recorded his first album in 1969 with Jerry Corbitt (of The Youngbloods fame) producing. It was released in 1970 on the Mediarts label after being turned down by 34 record companies. When it finally came out, *Tapestry* (released a year before the Carole King album of the same name) garnered excellent reviews and established McLean as a club headliner. In 1970 he also laboured to build the sloop "Clearwater," launched that year in Bristol, Maine, performing 30 concerts with Seeger to help meet the costs.

In late 1971 he released *American Pie* on United Artists and became the most successful "new" artist to break that year. The title song heralded the end of a musical era, and became a media event that reached far beyond the impact of a mere hit single; McLean's lyrics were analyzed and re-analyzed by *Life*, *Time* and *Newsweek*, as well as on radio and television and in publications around the world. McLean was nominated that year for four Grammy Awards (Best Album, Best Song, Best Record and Best Performance). Almost as amazing as the song "American Pie" was McLean's follow-up single, "Vincent," his stirring tribute to artist Vincent Van Gogh, that became an even larger international hit than "Pie."

In 1972, he released *Don McLean,* a reaction to the pressures and attention of sudden stardom. The album included the songs "Dreidel" and "If We Try," both strong chart singles. Soon weary of the gruelling schedule of world touring that followed "American Pie," McLean took a break from concert performing to play some low-key club gigs with mandolinist Frank Wakefield, which led to the album *Playin' Favorites,* an album of non-originals recorded in traditional folk, country and bluegrass styles. "Mountains of Mourne" from the LP became a number one single in Ireland, where McLean is a superstar, as he is in England,

where his rendition of Buddy Holly's "Everyday" from the same album hit the Top 10.

McLean released *Homeless Brother* in 1974, an album produced by Joel Dorn that offered nine new originals like "Wonderful Baby" (a number one Adult Contemporary single), a song inspired by Fred Astaire and later recorded by him, and "La La Love You," another chart single.
In 1976, he released *Solo,* a double-live album that captured the McLean solo concert experience, and included his haunting three-part singalong, "Babylon."

In late 1977, McLean released *Prime Time*, his first collection of new material in two and a half years.

Chain Lightning was released in 1981. An album with a 50/50 split of new McLean originals and classic pop songs like "Crying," (a top-5 hit on the pop, country and adult contemporary charts in American, as well as a number-one gold single in Holland and Britain) Gene Vincent's "Lotta Lovin'," Buddy Holly's "It Doesn't Matter Anymore," "Since I Don't Have You"(Top-20 on the pop, country and Adult Contemorary charts) and "It's Just the Sun" (which hit the Top-15 Adult Contemorary, and charted pop and country).

Chain Lightning signalled another milestone in McLean's relationship to American music, as well as his return to the top of the U.S. charts. On the heels of the album, McLean embarked on a British tour with a versatile six-piece rock 'n' roll band and a nine-piece string section, enabling him to perform a wide range of material in any format, followed by his first American tour with a full band, which featured Garth Hudson of the Band on keyboards and reeds and drummer Bob Henrit from the group Argent.

Throughout his career, Don McLean has toured the world primarily performing solo with his guitar and banjo, although he has been backed by everything from rock bands to bluegrass groups to symphony orchestras. The autumn and winter of

1981 found McLean headlining a 40-city tour of North America, backed by such musicians as Darius Brubeck (son of jazz great Dave Brubeck) on piano and John Platania (former Van Morrison guitar ace).

In 1982 McLean had the best year of his career, completing a sold out tour of sixteen countries and over 100 cities around the world, receiving gold and platinum albums for *The Very Best of Don McLean* (his 10th LP) in Australia, England and New Zealand while "Castles in the Air" climbed the U.S. charts and was one of the most played songs of the year. In addition, at his wrap up sold out concert at Carnegie Hall he was presented with his third "million Performance" certificate from BMI, making him one of only a handful of BMI writers to have received three or more such awards. 1982 also saw the release of *Believers*, produced by Larry Butler. In addition to three prime McLean cover versions — the Everly Brothers' and Roy Orbison's "Love Hurts," a heartfelt rendition of "Love Letters" and a rollicking "Sea Cruise," *Believers* contained McLean's most expansive collection of self-penned material to date.

1983 was spent preparing a comprehensive songbook of more than 60 McLean classics (published in 1984), a four month tour of the U.S.A. closing with his traditional Thanksgiving concert at Carnegie Hall featuring the Jordanaires. He also released *Dominion*, a two record, live LP recorded entirely at one performance, with rock orchestra, at the Dominion Theater.

After a few years hiatus, Don signed with Capitol Records and in 1986 released *Don McLean's Greatest Hits Then & Now*, a collection of 50% new songs and 50% McLean standards re-recorded, helping to re-introduce him to his old fans as well as gain many new ones.

In 1987 Don released *Love Tracks*, a straight ahead country album with songs from some of Nashville's top writers as well as a few new McLean originals.

Don McLean's latest release, *For the Memories Vol. 1 & 2* is his first for Gold Castle. Originally released only overseas, the project is a collection of over 20 songs, covering three decades of some of Don's favorite music. It carries the listener from the timeless music of Irving Berlin, George Gershwin and Cole Porter to the hits of Leiber and Stoller, Willie Nelson and Hank Williams. The sense of affection for this music is evident throughout, giving the record the feeling of a labor of love. As McLean writes in his liner notes, "many of these songs I have sung for years in concert, and some were done for these sessions, just for the memories."

Don McLean remains very active these days. His annual thanksgiving show at Carnegie Hall is already a sell-out and he plans to tour the U.K., typically selling out venues like London's Royal Albert Hall. American fans will also be hearing Don McLean in an upcoming PBS telecast on Vincent Van Gogh; in addition to featuring McLean's music, including his famous hit, "Vincent," the show will be narrated by the singer/songwriter as well.

Photo: David Gahr

AMERICAN PIE

Words and Music by
DON McLEAN

12

14

Additional Lyrics

2. Now for ten years we've been on our own,
   And moss grows fat on a rollin' stone
   But that's not how it used to be
   When the jester sang for the king and queen
   In a coat he borrowed from James Dean
   And a voice that came from you and me
   Oh and while the king was looking down,
   The jester stole his thorny crown
   The courtroom was adjourned,
   No verdict was returned
   And while Lenin read a book on Marx
   The quartet practiced in the park
   And we sang dirges in the dark
   The day the music died
   We were singin'... bye-bye... etc.

3. Helter-skelter in the summer swelter
   The birds flew off with a fallout shelter
   Eight miles high and fallin' fast,
   it landed foul on the grass
   The players tried for a forward pass,
   With the jester on the sidelines in a cast
   Now the half-time air was sweet perfume
   While the sergeants played a marching tune
   We all got up to dance
   But we never got the chance
   'Cause the players tried to take the field,
   The marching band refused to yield
   Do you recall what was revealed
   The day the music died
   We started singin'... bye-bye... etc.

4. And there we were all in one place,
   A generation lost in space
   With no time left to start again
   So come on, Jack be nimble, Jack be quick,
   Jack Flash sat on a candlestick
   'Cause fire is the devil's only friend
   And as I watched him on the stage
   My hands were clenched in fists of rage
   No angel born in hell
   Could break that Satan's spell
   And as the flames climbed high into the night
   To light the sacrificial rite
   I saw Satan laughing with delight
   The day the music died
   He was singin'... bye-bye... etc.

AND I LOVE YOU SO

Words and Music by
DON McLEAN

CASTLES IN THE AIR

Words and Music by
DON McLEAN

Save me _____ from all the trou - ble and the

pain. I know I'm weak, but I can't

face that girl a - gain. _____

Tell her _____ the rea - son

CROSSROADS

Words and Music by
DON McLEAN

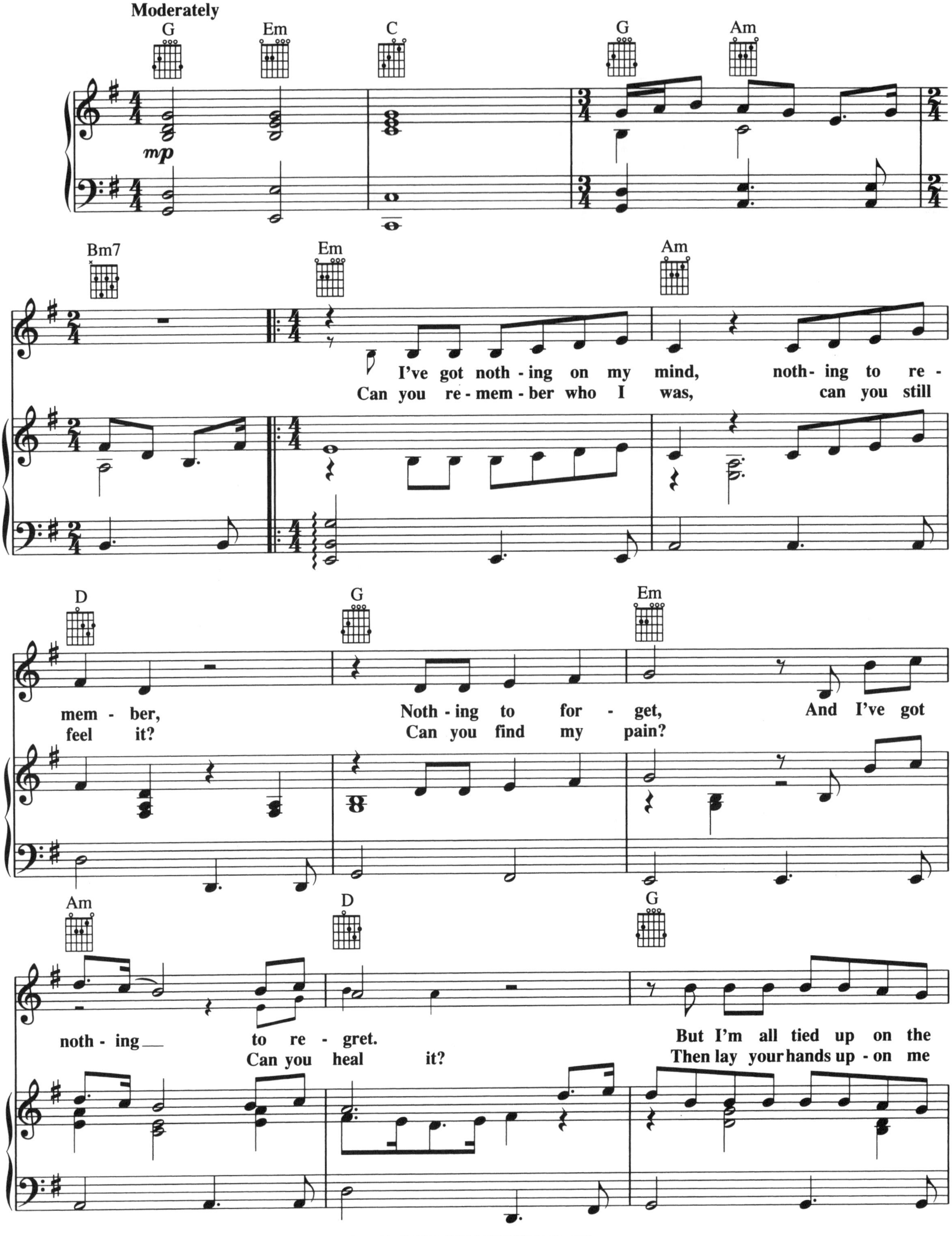

I've got noth-ing on my mind, noth-ing to re-

Can you re-mem-ber who I was, can you still

mem-ber,

feel it?

Noth-ing to for-get,

Can you find my get, pain?

And I've got

noth-ing ___ to re-gret.

Can you heal it?

But I'm all tied up on the

Then lay your hands up-on me

25

Don McLean with wife, Patrisha and baby daughter, Jacqueline Lee.

Photo Credit: Peter Nash

EMPTY CHAIRS

Words and Music by
DON McLEAN

EVERYBODY LOVES ME, BABY

Words and Music by
DON McLEAN

Additional Lyrics

2. The purist race I've bred for thee,
   To live in my democracy;
   The highest human pedigree awaits your
       first born boy baby.

   My face on every coin engraved,
   The anarchists are all enslaved;
   My own flag is forever waved
       by the grateful people I have saved
   You see, *(Chorus)*

3. No land is beyond my claim,
   When land is seized in the people's name;
   By evil men who rob and maim,
   If war is hell, I'm not to blame.

   Why you can't blame me, I'm Heaven's child,
   I'm the second son of Mary mild;
   And twice removed from Oscar Wilde,
   But he didn't mind, why he just smiled.
   You see, *(Chorus)*

4. Now the ocean parts when I walk through,
   The clouds dissolve, the sky turns blue;
   I'm held in very great value by
   Everyone I meet but you.

   'Cause I've used my talents as I could
   I've done some bad, I've done some good;
   I did a whole lot better than they thought I could,
   Some come on and treat me like you should.
   Because *(Chorus)*

MAGDALENE LANE

Words and Music by
DON McLEAN

40

43

ORPHANS OF WEALTH

Words and Music by
DON McLEAN

There is no time —
come from the north —

— to dis - cuss or de - bate — what is right, what is wrong for our
— and they come from the south — and they come from the hills — and the

peo - ple. — Time has run out for all those who
val - leys. — And they're mi - grants and farm - ers and min - ers who and

50

floods in the nurse-ry and a child ___ is cry-ing. He's hun-gry and cold. _____ His life has been sold. His young face looks old. ___ It's the face of A-mer-i-ca dy-ing.

rit.

Additional Lyrics

And with roaches and rickets and rats in the thickets
Infested diseased and decaying
With rags and no shoes and skin sores that ooze
By the poisonous pools they are playing
In shacks of two rooms that are rotting wood tombs
With corpses breathing inside them
And we pity their plight as they call in the night
And we do all that we can to hide them.

Chorus (Coda)

RESPECTABLE

Words and Music by
DON McLEAN

56

TAPESTRY

Words and Music by
DON McLEAN

1. Ev - 'ry thread of cre -
2.-5. *See additional lyrics*

a - tion is held in po - si - tion by still oth - er strands of things

liv - ing; In an earth - ly tap - es - try hung from the

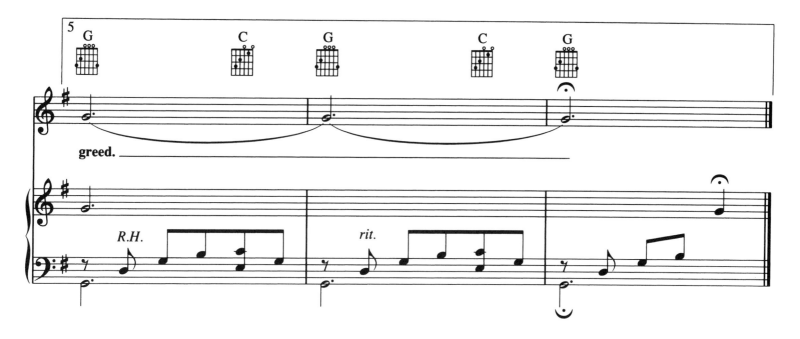

greed. _____

Additional Lyrics

2. Every breeze that blows kindly is one crystal breath,
   We exhale on the blue diamond heaven;
   As gentle to touch as the hands of the healer,
   As soft as farewells whispered over the coffin,
   We're poisoned by venom with each breath we take,
   From the brown sulphur chimney
   And the black highway snake.

3. Every dawn that breaks golden is held in suspension,
   Like the yolk of the egg in albumen;
   Where the birth and the death of unseen generations,
   Are interdependent in vast orchestration,
   And painted in colors of tapestry thread,
   When the dying are born and the living are dead.

4. Every pulse of your heartbeat is one liquid moment,
   That flows through the veins of your being;
   Like a river of life flowing on since creation,
   Approaching the sea with each new generation,
   You're now just a stagnant and rancid disgrace,
   That is rapidly drowning the whole human race.

5. Every fish that swims silent, every bird
        that flies freely,
   Every doe that steps softly;
   Every crisp leaf that falls, all the flowers that grow,
   On this colorful tapestry, somehow they know,
   That if man is allowed to destroy all we need,
   He will soon have to pay with his life
   For his greed.

THREE FLIGHTS UP

Words and Music by
DON McLEAN

69

72

TILL TOMORROW

Words and Music by
DON McLEAN

VINCENT
(STARRY STARRY NIGHT)

Words and Music by
DON McLEAN

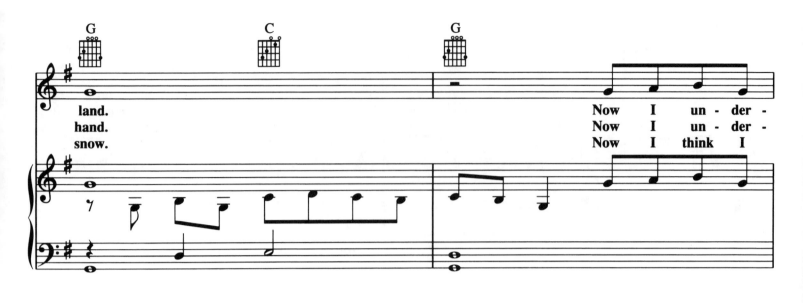

land.
hand.
snow.

Now I un - der -
Now I un - der -
Now I think I

stand
stand
know

what you tried to say to me,
what you tried to say to me,
what you tried to say to me,

How you suf - fered for your san - i - ty,
How you suf - fered for your san - i - ty,
How you suf - fered for your san - i - ty,

How you tried to set them
How you tried to set them
How you tried to set them

WINTERWOOD

Words and Music by
DON McLEAN

D I S C O G R A P H Y

SINGLES

CASTLES IN THE AIR / AND I LOVE YOU SO — Mediarts (1969)
AMERICAN PIE / AMERICAN PIE (continued) — United Artists (1971)
VINCENT / CASTLES IN THE AIR — United Artists (1972)
DREIDEL / BRONCO BILL'S LAMENT — United Artists (1972)
IF WE TRY / THE MORE YOU PAY (The More It's Worth) — United Artists (1973)
FOOL'S PARADISE / HAPPY TRAILS — United Artists (1973)
MOUNTAINS OF MOURNE / BILL CHEATHAM - OLD JOE CLARK — United Artists (1973)
EVERYDAY (non LP, live from BBC) / THE MORE YOU PAY (THE MORE IT'S WORTH) — United Artists (UK) (1973)
SITTING ON TOP OF THE WORLD / MULESKINNER BLUES — United Artists (1973)
WONDERFUL BABY / BIRTHDAY SONG — United Artists (1974)
PRIME TIME / WHEN A GOOD THING GOES BAD — Arista (1977)
IT DOESN'T MATTER ANYMORE / IF WE TRY (non LP) — Arista (1978)
CRYING / GENESIS (IN THE BEGINNING) — Millennium (1981)
LLORAS (Crying in Spanish) / GENESIS — EMI (Spain) (1981)
SINCE I DON'T HAVE YOU / YOUR CHEATING HEART — Millennium (1981)
IT'S JUST THE SUN / CHAIN LIGHTNING — Millennium (1981)
YO SOY TU ERES (It's Just The Sun in Spanish) / CHAIN LIGHTNING — EMI (Spain) (1981)
CASTLES IN THE AIR (new version) / CRAZY EYES — Millennium (1981)
JERUSALEM / LEFT FOR DEAD ON THE ROAD OF LOVE — Millennium (1981)
JERUSALEM (film version) — Columbia (Israel) (1981)
L'AFFAIR D'AMOUR (non LP) — JERUSALEM / Interfusion (Australia) (1984)
HE'S GOT YOU — Capitol (1986)
SUPERMAN'S GHOST — Capitol (1987)
EVENTUALLY — Capitol (1988)
LOVE IN MY HEART — Capitol (1989)
MAYBE BABY — Interfusion (1989 - Australia)

ALBUMS

TAPESTRY — Mediarts (1969) and United Artists (1972)
AMERICAN PIE — United Artists (1971)
DON MCLEAN — United Artists (1972)
PLAYIN' FAVORITES — United Artists (1973)
HOMELESS BROTHER — United Artists (1974)
SOLO — United Artists (1976)
PRIME TIME — Arista (1977)
CHAIN LIGHTNING — Millennium (1981)
BELIEVERS — Millennium (1981)
DOMINION — EMI-UK (1983) Re-release Gold Castle - U.S.A. (1990)
GREATEST HITS, THEN AND NOW — Capitol - EMI (1988)
LOVE TRACKS — Capitol - EMI (1989)
FOR THE MEMORIES (Vol. 1 & 2) — Gold Castle (1990)

(As A Featured Artist):
CLEARWATER — Clearwater (1974)
CLEARWATER — Clearwater (1977)